THE REACTIVATED MAN

Curtis Zahn

BROADWAY PLAY PUBLISHING INC
224 E 62nd St, NY, NY 10065
www.broadwayplaypub.com
info@broadwayplaypub.com

THE REACTIVATED MAN
© Copyright 1982 Curtis Zahn

All rights reserved. This work is fully protected under the copyright laws of the United States of America. No part of this publication may be photocopied, reproduced, stored in a retrieval system, or transmitted, in any form or by any means, electronic, mechanical, recording, or otherwise, without the prior permission of the publisher. Additional copies of this play are available from the publisher.

Written permission is required for live performance of any sort. This includes readings, cuttings, scenes, and excerpts. For amateur and stock performances, please contact Broadway Play Publishing Inc. For all other rights please contact the author's estate c/o B P P I.

Cover art by Jamie Lustberg

First edition: April 1984
This edition: October 2017
I S B N: 978-0-88145-014-9

Text from *West Coast Plays 11/12*

The Reactivated Man was first presented at the Edward Ludlum Theatre in Los Angeles in April of 1965 with the following cast:

NILES	Joseph Donte
NURSE	Rebecca Evans
PAULA	Jean Field
NORM	Herschel Reiter
SLEEVE	Charles Thompson

Directed by Frank Bolger

SETTING

A dimly lit adobe in disrepair, near the sea, alone, and lighted only by candles and kerosene lamps. At center stage there is a set of French windows and a table. An operating table is at stage left.

TIME

The present. Whatever year it is at the time of performance. This text has updated certain topical references to 1982. Further updating should be carried out as required.

The Reactivated Man
Curtis Zahn

Two doctors are hovering over CHARLES NILES *on the operating table.* PAULA NILES *and the* NURSE *sit at a table by window where coffee heats over a candle. Low moody lighting.*

NILES: (*A poetic, slow, and sad monotone narration which he will use throughout play during his "recounting."*) For the duration of that hushed, hesitant, ominous night they kept taking it apart and putting it back together again, while a shy moon came and went, and an abusive surf thundered above the cries of marsh birds in the great swamp.

Idly, the NURSE *has pushed open the french window, flooding room with the theme song played on a nickelodeon.*

NORM: (*Sharply.*) Nurse! (*The* NURSE *closes window; music faint again.*)

SLEEVE: (*To* NORM.) He's going out again, Norm.

NORM: Yes, yes, of course, J.E.

SLEEVE: It didn't take so much.

NORM: (*Argumentatively.*) And again . . . it *might* take much *more.*

SLEEVE: (*Rising.*) That's more or less what I said! (*Pause.*) More!

NORM: (*He stops work and faces* SLEEVE. *Heatedly.*) Not at all! You said *less!* More than two hours ago you said *less!*

SLEEVE: *Wrong! That was more or less before we gave* him *more!* (PAULA *registers concern at their bickering; the* NURSE *stolidly chews gum.*)

NORM: Earlier!

SLEEVE: *Later!* We gave him *less.* (*A pause.*) *Then* more!

NORM: (*Starts to swing his Phi Beta Kappa key.*) I'm sorry! It's the *other* way 'round!

NORM: *Which* way?

SLEEVE: The *other* other way!

NORM: (*In a fury.*) *Other* other way! What kind of talk is that? I merely said . . . (*Pause.*) Then you said . . . (*Pause.*) Which compelled me to . . . (*The* NURSE *knocks a bottle off table. The splintering crash halts them.* NORM *wipes off a dripping morsel and starts to work.*) I'll hear no more about it! The more you rationalize, the less I listen!

SLEEVE: (*Starting to work.*) Agreed! And the *less* you listen, the *more* I realize you know *more* about *less* than anyone I know. (*He picks up an enormous electric drill and starts to hold it against* NILES's *head, then changes his mind.*)

NILES: I had come here for an operation of a most unusual and delicate nature. (*A pause. Then table swings around and he pops up facing the audience.*) I had finally decided to have it removed. That is, *Paula* had decided for me! (*Hot spot on* PAULA.)

PAULA: (*She leaps up as lights over operating area diminish and spot remains in her area.*) Charles! That's not *exactly* true!

NURSE: (*Calls to* NILES.) That's just like an abortion or anything else, sweetie!

PAULA: (*To* NURSE.) His name is Charles!

NURSE: Charley?! (*Now expansively.*) *Chuck!*

SLEEVE: You got hemorrhoids, you have them removed. Charlie!

NORM: Or another example . . . a retroactive esophagus!

NURSE: Or excessive *hair!* I used to have *loads* of it, Chuck! (*A beat.*) So you go to a doc to have anything removed you never wanted in the second place!

SLEEVE: Or a wisdom tooth! If you're smart, you get rid of wisdom tooths! (*Pause.*) Teeth!

NILES: (*Theme music rises, now in poetic recall again.*) They were all propping each other up with explanations and rationalizations. The doctor they referred to as "J.E." was named Sleeve. Doctor Sleeve, I presume. (*Light comes up on* SLEEVE. *He makes a modest bow.*) The other's name I never knew. He was just "Norm." And in a way he represented it — the norm.

NORM: (*Light comes up on him. He bows, then assumes a lecture stance, twirling his fraternity key.*) Uh . . . you can have your guilts removed two ways! Through psychoanalysis, as is well known, but which sometimes takes months or years, and it is . . . expensive—

NURSE: (*Exuberantly cuts him off.*) And half the time those darn old guilts just flare up again at some future time! (*She accidentally knocks a clock off the table, picks it up.*)

SLEEVE: (*Ignoring her scene.*) The other way is fairly new! A surgical operation on that part of the brain lobe where overactive guilts produce excruciating anxieties—

NURSE: (*Exuberantly cutting in again.*) There's a third way, Chuck . . . but . . . (*Pause, voice drops.*) I . . . I already tried it!

SLEEVE: Nurse!
NURSE: (*Apologizing.*) I was only going to tell him about heroin . . . (*Pause.*) and acid.
NILES: (*Weakly.*) What about them?
PAULA: Oh, Charles!
NURSE: They don't work. Because I used to be a hippy and . . . (*She pauses, realizing that* PAULA *is looking at her with incredulous interest.*) I mean, shit! I tried speed and grass . . . You name it!
NORM: Nurse!
NURSE: (*Impassioned.*) I'm telling it like it isn't! (*Pause.*) I mean, wasn't! The trip only lasts *a while!* Less than that, even! Then you're right back where you started—simply *loaded with guilts!*
PAULA: (*A pause; quietly.*) And this way is . . . permanent?
SLEEVE: Forever!
PAULA: And no . . . side effects?
NURSE: (*Enthusiastic.*) Look at me! Norm operated on me way back in *1971!* (*She bumps into a table, almost upsetting its contents. A weak, self-conscious smile now.*) Reflex action! (*Pause.*) I always do that when I think about 1971. (*The doctors force a laugh; she straightens the table. Theme music loudens again.*)
NILES: I listened to the marsh-birds cackling . . . sharing the joke. I heard the carnival music, braving the fog in some old forgotten seaport. (*Pause.*) And I suddenly heard Paula's doubts, beating around her eyes and ears. She said:
PAULA: (*To doctors.*) But you have to admit it's, well, it's not . . . natural.
SLEEVE: *Natural?*
NORM: So what's natural nowadays.
SLEEVE: Twentieth-century man is an automobile junk yard of surplus parts!
NURSE: Like I said! God gave me surplus hair . . . (*Pause.*) But no boobs!
SLEEVE: Nurse!
NURSE: So I had the former removed and the latter installed! (*Brightly.*) Norm fixed me with a matched pair! (*To* PAULA.) Incidentally, honey . . . if you aren't satisfied with the way God made you . . .
SLEEVE: (*Sternly, to* NURSE.) Miss Thanatopsis!
NURSE: (*Apologetically to* PAULA.) It's not God's fault! *Eveybody* makes mistakes! (NURSE *waits; doctors observe* PAULA *interestedly.*)

PAULA: *(Shakes head.)* Thank you. I . . .
NILES: *(Facing* PAULA.*)* She's perfectly satisfied—aren't you, Paula?
PAULA: Well . . . *(Pause.)* I . . . I haven't given the matter much thought. *(Smiles, gestures.)* Besides! It gives you an incentive to try harder . . . (NURSE *knocks another object over.*)
NORM: *(Tired, scolding tone.)* Nurse!
SLEEVE: *(A pause. Music swells.)* Uh, Mr. Niles . . . *(Another pause.)* What's your first name, Niles? Charles?
NURSE: Chuck!
SLEEVE: Chuck! Chuck, you should understand we're all here to carry on where nature left off . . . finish the job.
NORM: *(Cheerily.)* Add a little bit here, subtract a little there.
NURSE: And the brain's no different from the rest of the physiological body! Here we are in the present century and we got all those obsolete parts! An over-active recall. An incipient guilt lobe! *(Pause.)* I was simply loaded with guilts till I met Norm. *(Pause, now wildly.)* I couldn't even go to the bathroom if somebody was watching!!

Doctors show embarrassment. NILES, *for the first time, begins to get half off the table to say something, to stare at everyone.* PAULA *gets up, opens window pensively. The carnival music instantly floods room.*

SLEEVE: *(Assuming* NURSE *opened window.)* Nurse! *(Sees that it was* PAULA.*)* Oh, excuse me, Mrs. . . . Mrs. . . .
PAULA: *(Closes window.)* Niles. Paula Niles, who tries harder!
NORM: I'm sorry, Mrs. Niles. We have to exercise every precaution.
PAULA: I know. The operation is illegal.
NILES: Illegal and *unnatural!*
NURSE: Well, of course, it's illegal, sweetie! Merely because AMA is aways fifty years behind the future! Reactionary old fogies!
NORM: All brain surgery was illegal once upon a time, Chuck!
NURSE: More recent than that even!
SLEEVE: *Abortions* were illegal!
NURSE: *(To* PAULA.*)* Incidentally, we used to do them too, until it . . . until it . . .
PAULA: Became legal?
NURSE: *(Drops a test tube.) No!* I mean, *sure!* *(Pause.)* Well, doctors have got to make a living just like everybody else. *(Inspired.)* There's no *challenge* in abortions! You see, Norm and J.E. are

pioneers! They like to play around with the hidden, dark recesses of the mind! They're *hooked* on the *unknown!*
PAULA: (*Worried.*) The unknown?
NILES: Paula! I thought you said—
SLEEVE: Miss Thanatopsis. (*More sternly.*) Miss Thanatopsis!
NORM: All she's saying—
SLEEVE: She's simply pointing out that the medical fraternity is afraid of the human brain, sir.
NORM: Won't touch it!
SLEEVE: Unless it's some poor psychopath already headed for the electric chair!
NURSE: Or some homo they caught banging little kids!
SLEEVE: She means . . . (*Pause.*) The point is . . .
NURSE: Siegfried Frood was a pioneer! Only, instead of going in there with words, Norm and J.E. use a darn little old drill and an ear scoop!
SLEEVE: And it's permanent.
NORM: You don't keep coming back for therapy and forking over all the bread.
SLEEVE: He means—
NURSE: He means, the whole bottom's going to drop out of Froodian psychology some fine day!
NORM: It's a put on.
SLEEVE: A rip-off! (*Pause; now gravely.*) I'd be the last to disparage my esteemed colleague. However—
NORM: However, we know several psychologists who have just as many guilts as Chuck.
NURSE: For charging all that money!
NORM: *They* come to *us!*
SLEEVE: (*To* PAULA.) For the same, simple alteration we're performing on your husband.
NURSE: Actually, Norm and J.E. are heroes! (*Inspired.*) They could be *arrested* for what they're doing!
NORM: (*Modestly.*) Oh, come! Miss Thanatopsis!
SLEEVE: We just don't like to see beautiful people suffer! That is all.
NORM: We happen to believe in what we are doing. That is all.
NURSE: (*Reverently.*) There've always been martyrs in the world! Look at Lenny Bruce! Jesus Christ! (*Pause.*) *Sun Moon!* The Almighty works in mysterious ways. (*The window blows open, flooding the room with a crescendo of carnival music. All stare at the phenomena.* PAULA *calmly goes over and closes it.*)

SLEEVE: Uh, Niles — I mean Charles. You've had psychotherapy, right?
NORM: And it didn't help. Right?
PAULA: No!
NILES: Yes!
SLEEVE: Which?
NORM: Yes or no?
NILES: No! I mean, *yes!*
PAULA: No.
NURSE: They mean, after you spend all that money you still got guilts! (*To* NILES.) Huh? (*To* PAULA.) Huh?
NORM: Put it this way, Mrs . . .
PAULA: Paula Niles, who tries harder.
NORM: Paula — you got an earache you don't go to a headshrinker.
NILES: (*Weakly, far away.*) Maybe you do!
NURSE: Or a ruminating trombolises! Guilt is actually a disease! Like syphilis or anything else!
NILES: (*A wail.*) I don't *have* a guilt complex! (*The* NURSE *drops another bottle. The doctors stand aghast.*)
SLEEVE: According to patient's case-history, he was virtually immobilized by guilts. (PAULA *and* NILES *shake their heads.*)
NORM: Patient was unable to cope with environment in normal manner.
NURSE: Can't eat Kentucky Fried Chicken without he throws up!
PAULA: Neither can I. Is that abnormal?
NILES: Besides . . . we're vegetarians.
PAULA: For humanitarian reasons.
NURSE: You're both confusing me! Humanitarians don't eat chickens — right? Then why do vegetarians eat vegetables?
SLEEVE: Nurse! Bring me patient's behavior pattern.
NILES: I don't *have* a pattern.
NURSE: That's right, Charlie! (*To* SLEEVE.) He does everything ass backwa- . . . I mean . . . (*Impetuously inspired.*) He *improvises!*
SLEEVE & NORM: (*In unison.*) He what?
PAULA: My husband — he has to stop and think about everything. He —
NURSE: (*To doctors.*) Practically everything *you* do, he shouldn't! (*The doctors appear offended.*) Chuck believes in *honesty!* (*They are more offended.*) He believes in *humanitarianism* — despite he eats vegetables.
NILES: There is a difference between guilt and conscience.

The Reactivated Man

NURSE: Chuck gives it away to the poor! (*Pause.*) Money, not sex!
SLEEVE: The point is —
NORM: The point is —
NILES: Let me explain. Guilt is —
PAULA: Oh, Charles.
NURSE: Sweetie! We're all trying to help you!
NILES: I just want to explain one thing.
PAULA: Charles, you've explained it all a thousand times! To me! To the children! The neighbors! The income tax collector.
NILES: Paula —
PAULA: Explaining doesn't buy shoes for the children! Explaining doesn't meet the payments on the house.
NILES: Paula! The house was your idea in the first place!
PAULA: But you agreed to it!
NILES: And I agreed to come *here*. Nevertheless . . .
PAULA: Nevertheless our bank account is overdrawn again. Why? Because you can't conscientiously do this kind of work! Or that kind of work! Because it might be dishonest or helping the war! Or — (*She breaks off conversation.*)
NURSE: (*To* PAULA.) I know just how you feel. I had several boyfriends that didn't believe in work! Dozens!
NILES: I do believe in work! Paula means —
NURSE: He means work that doesn't hurt anybody!
SLEEVE: What kind —
NORM: Is that?
NURSE: Work that doesn't cause war. Or violence. Charley wouldn't hurt a flea — right? (*Glance at* NILES.)
SLEEVE: Wouldn't?
NORM: (*Moves menacingly to* NILES.) Not even if it came up and bit you?
SLEEVE: (*Makes as though to slap* NILES.) Not even if it bit you?
NURSE: He'd turn the other cheek!
SLEEVE: Which cheek?
NURSE: He's one of *those*. He don't believe in violence.
SLEEVE: Oh! (*To* NORM.) He's one of *those!*
NORM: I heard you. (*Threateningly.*) Mr Niles! Suppose I started to hit you! What would you say?
NILES: I'd say, (*Pause.*) please don't.
NORM: That's all?
NILES: I think so. (*Pause.*) Yes!
SLEEVE: You wouldn't hit back?

NILES: (*After a pause.*) No, sir, I . . . I . . .
NURSE: (*Enthralled.*) He's *really* sick!
PAULA: As you said, he is one of those. (*Pause.*) So am I. At least we have that in common. (*All are caught by surprise as* SLEEVE *slaps* NILES. NILES *recoils. But makes no effort to retaliate.* PAULA *watches very calmly.* NURSE *is shocked.*)
NORM: You wouldn't even defend yourself? (*He slaps* NILES. NILES *ducks, trying to avoid being struck, but shows no anger, only pain. Both doctors alternately hit* NILES. *However, now they seem weary of the game.*)
NURSE: He's really got it bad.
SLEEVE: Most advanced case I've ever seen! (*As a final test, he whirls, as though to strike* NILES *again.* NILES *stoically faces him.*)
NORM: Obviously, psychoanalysis didn't help at all. (*He also starts to strike* NILES.)
SLEEVE: Obviously!
NURSE: Obviously!
NILES: (*A wounded shout.*) But it *did!* (*All turn around, startled.*) I got rid of certain *guilts*.
NORM: Then, why, may I ask . . . ?
NURSE: Sweetie! You're not coming clean!
NILES: But, then, there was this *new* guilt.
SLEEVE: It is my absolute understanding —
NILES: (*He waves them silent.*) I know! But then, there was this *new guilt!* (*Impatient, impassioned.*) The *cost!* (*He tries to climb off table; they work at restraining him.*) Have *I* the right to spend sixty-five dollars an hour on psychiatry when other people are *really* sick? Or hungry?
SLEEVE: (*A pause; now with mock cheer.*) Well! That's a new angle!
NURSE: You go to a head-shrinker to get cured of one thing, and —
NORM: Exactly! I have always steadfastly maintained consistently —
SLEEVE: Exactly! But *who* are these hungry people, Charley?
NORM: Yes! Quite! But where are they? Do you see any, J.E.?
SLEEVE: Not at all! I see rich, pampered bastards trying to overthrow the government.
NORM: Ever see a hippie that wasn't getting unemployment insurance? (*Pause.*) Miss Thanatopsis, do you know any poor people in dire need of medical attention?
NURSE: (*Holds up a finger.*) Only one! That's why I didn't marry him.

The Reactivated Man

NORM: Where are these people, Mr. Niles?
NILES: Everywhere! The people who live on the other side of the billboards. (*Doctors and* NURSE *look to* PAULA *for an explanation.*)
PAULA: My husband feels —
NILES: (*Cutting her off.*) Two-thirds of the world is underfed! There is *one* doctor for every million persons! (*Affixes glance on* SLEEVE. *Now looks accusingly at* NURSE. *Hysterical shout.*) There is a critical population explosion!
NURSE: Don't look at me, Sweetie. (PAULA *goes back to table by window.*)
NILES: (*To all of them.*) There's but one reason I'm here! Your operation is cheaper than psychoanalysis.
NURSE: Or heroin, Sweetie.
NORM: (*Swinging his key.*) You want to be rid of nagging guilts?
SLEEVE: You remove that small knob on the brain that causes the trouble. (*He holds up a jar and points.*)
NORM: From the *northeast* section of the brain. Smack in front of your anti-cerebellum unicoxus.
SLEEVE: Just south of the homo intellectus. (NILES *and* PAULA *hear the words with dutiful doubt.* NORM *swats a fly. They observe this also.*)
NURSE: (*Demonstrates with fingers.*) No bigger than a mosquito bite! (*Joyous wonder.*) Under the microscope it looks like a tangled-up tiny portion of spaghetti with clam sauce!
SLEEVE: (*Noting that* PAULA *and* NILES *recoil.*) Nurse! Bring me a recall.
NURSE: (*Heading for mantel where jars are lined up.*) Yes sir. (*To* NILES, *over the shoulder.*) Yet a great weight's been lifted right off your mind!
NORM: (*Swats at another fly.*) All of us have had ours removed.
SLEEVE: *All* of us. Actually, Miss Thanatopsis' was over-enlarged. Size of a cockroach!
NURSE: (*Returning with jar.*) Because I hated my parents.
PAULA: (*Newly interested.*) And you don't hate them now?
NURSE: (*Shakes her head violently.*) I never *think* of them now. (*The window blows open again, bringing the carnival music in loudly.* NURSE *crosses and closes it.*)
SLEEVE: (*Philosophically.*) It used to bother me, seeing sickness and poverty.
NURSE: Me too. I used to cry *daily*. Even after I dropped out.
NORM: It is man's destiny that his world shall always be filled with

trouble. To survive, one must protect oneself, physically *and* mentally!

PAULA: (*Jumps up agitatedly.*) But we know all this! (*To* NURSE.) Everything's been settled! Why are we standing here talking?

Impulsively, she turns and opens window. No music. Only sounds of frogs, surf, marsh birds, crickets. Lights go out briefly. Marsh sounds continue as NILES *narrates.*

NILES: (*Poetic "narrative" tone.*) And so, while the doctors labored over me, my innermost thoughts came and went under a counterpoint of frogs and carnival music while strange faces scowled in the flickering light. (*Part laughingly.*) It isn't quite true that I'd agreed to having my soul shorted-out. My conscious mind said "yes." The tongue. The lips. And I believe the latter smiled even. But deep in the subconscious, that bathospheric volcano of righteousness, there was resistance. It was this they were after.

Nickleodeon music erupts; it is suggestive of Victorian bordello piano jazz. Strobe lights produce a "quickie" effect like old time movies. Doctors move with exaggerated speed as they drill, saw, pound the patient. NURSE *moves jerkily to and fro, carrying things; at the end of refrain, entire company freezes as a still-life.*

NORM: (*Excitedly.*) I think we've got it this time, J.E.! Really I do!
SLEEVE: Of course!
NORM: Really I do! I really think we've got it!
NURSE: (*Gloriously.*) Oh, doctor!
SLEEVE: (*Peering inside skull.*) There it is! It was right there all the time. Next to the libido!
NORM: The libido was over-active!
NURSE: They always are! Remember that used car salesman? I never—
NORM: (*Cuts her off.*) Nurse! Did you sterilize my wire cutters?!
NURSE: Natch! And the pliers.
SLEEVE: (*Stands back, waits.*) Well? Now?
NORM: (*Lights cigarette.*) I . . . I thought I'd make a few exploratory probes first.
NURSE: (*Nods emphatically.*) We got loads of time! It's only four AM.
SLEEVE: (*Lowers voice.*) Obviously it's going to be difficult to get past the patient's *recall.*
NORM: (*A cautious glance at* PAULA, *who appears to be asleep sitting up.*) Obviously.

The Reactivated Man

NURSE: (*Peering into* NILES's *skull again.*) It's a whopper if I ever saw one.
NORM: (*Lowered voice, watching* PAULA.) I thought I'd circumvent his memory by going in close to the motor nerves. (*Coughs.*) Of course, I'd use my number four iron. I'd follow through with clamps.
SLEEVE: (*Cautioning.*) And if the motor nerves—?
NURSE: (*To* SLEEVE, *a worried whisper.*) Remember what happened to that broker?
SLEEVE: (*Leans closer to her;* NORM *cannot hear but is suspicious.*) Eh?
NURSE: (*Whispers with a cautious glance at* PAULA.) That tall fellow from Pierce, Fenner, Merill, Lynch and whoever it is. Something got shorted out. Every time he rode in a taxi, he urinated.
NORM: (*Overhears; angry.*) Nurse! Bring me the micrometer! (*To* SLEEVE.) You have to take risks. Nothing ventured leaves a guilt complex running 'round.
NURSE: Too much conscience makes a dull boy! (*Lowered voice.*) His wife says they're absolutely overrun with mice.
NORM: (*Questioningly.*) MMmmmmmmmmmm?
NURSE: (*To* NORM.) He can't kill anything! Too *conscientious*. (*Pause.*) And he's failing in business.
NORM: (*Sarcastically.*) Imagine! J.E.!
NURSE: (*Oblivious to his tone, nods vehemently.*) And they had to borrow on their house!
NORM: (*Mocking sternness.*) Doctor Sleeve! Am I to understand from this ravishing young creature that the Horatio Alger success story no longer works? (NURSE, *embarrassed, drops hammer.*)
SLEEVE: (*Professing alarm.*) It sounds extremely un-American! I was taught that honesty and virtue were second only to charity!
NURSE: (*She catches on, but is determined to go on with her point.*) She said he lost forty-five hundred last month. Turned down a big deal because it sounded dishonest! They got three kids and a beat-up old Chevy station wagon and she may have to go to work.
NORM: J.E.! This should be reported to the President!
SLEEVE: Or the FBI! It sounds suspicous to begin with.
NORM: Honest *business man!* Must be from some retarded country!
SLEEVE: Typical charity case. Doesn't know how to lie or cheat!
NURSE: (*Stubbornly.*) As a matter of fact, she said he *gives* a lot of their money to charity. I mean, do-gooder causes.

NORM: Diseased conscience. Used to be a familiar type around here.
SLEEVE: (*Laughs.*) Nowadays they just get ulcers. Or cancer . . .
NORM: (*Laughs.*) Or swallow happiness pills.
SLEEVE: (*Laughs.*) Or attach a hose to the exhaust pipe.
NORM: (*Rising laughter.*) Or endow a medical foundation.
NURSE: (*Laughter.*) Or join the Republican Party.
SLEEVE: (*Laughter.*) Or the Communist Party!
NURSE: (*Laughter.*) Like that engineer from Passaic! After the operation he became a White Muslim. (*All laugh loudly;* PAULA *awakes but they don't notice.*)
NORM: (*Mock seriousness.*) Of course *some* businessmen can just turn off their conscience until *after* they've made their killing.
NURSE: (*Laughter.*) And *then* jump out the window!
SLEEVE: (*Laughter, tears.*) And into the pscho ward . . .
NORM: (*Hysterical laughter, tears.*) Stopping to see a head-shrinker on the way down.

They figuratively roll with laughter. PAULA *stands up, opens window. Instantly the nickelodeon music drowns out the laughter and lights go out.*

NILES: (*Poetic narrator recount, vaguely.*) One seems to move horizontally in and out of worlds that ignore each other; time returns delicately, and begins to feel its way backwards into memory. (*Pause.*) And the listener stands, while archaeology goes by, throwing over its shoulder those things which were good or evil, or guilty and frightened, or shameful and triumphant.
   The doctors had pulled my past into the future and would freeze it there while Paula prepared for the thaw. A new part of me had invented anger now, and this was directed at my wife. (*Pause; spiritedly.*) Yes! The operation was her doing! I *had* to blame *someone!*
NORM: (*Quickly, loudly.*) Only the insane man blames himself! It's *normal* to blame others, eh, J.E.?
SLEEVE: Right! (*Humorously.*) And I'm going to blame *you* if the patient's motor nerves get fouled up!
NORM: (*Humorously.*) So, do I care? (*Pause. Coyly.*) That is, unless the operation you performed on *me* wasn't entirely successful!
NURSE: (*Good-humoredly.*) In which case you can blame *him!* (*Indicating* SLEEVE.)

The Reactivated Man

SLEEVE: (*Humorously.*) And *I* don't care, unless Norm's little job on me didn't do all it's supposed to do.

NILES: (*Narration, but thoughtful, questioningly.*) But what about Paula? I seemed to be lying there, watching love drift away while images of other girls, other times, crowded in, smiling.

NURSE: (*Crowding in, smiling.*) It'll all be over soon, Charley!

NILES: (*Stirs suddenly, addresses this directly to the* NURSE.) Some day I'll meet you in a cocktail lounge and neither of us will recognize myself. (NURSE's *smile freezes embarrassedly, then returns in force, but with a glance at* PAULA.)

SLEEVE: (*Quickly to* NURSE.) What's he saying?

NILES: (*Sits up quickly; in a declaration.*) Paula will have to have hers out, too! (*All four attentive.*) The operation! (NILES *waves a scalpel which alarms all.*) Otherwise she'll suffer! She'll have guilts for talking *me* into it. (*Jumps off table.*) She'll have to have *hers* remo-...

NURSE: (*Interrupts—; takes his arm.*) Sweetie! (*Coaxing him back.*) It's okay to blow your top but you got to take it easy!

SLEEVE: (*Cryptically.*) The top of your head's over there on the mantel!

NURSE: And your recall.

NORM: (*Sharply.*) Nurse! Did you remember to put his recall up there next to his memory? (NURSE *knocks over a lighted candle.*)

NURSE: I forgot. Sorry. (NURSE *picks up candle, races over to mantel with another jar, places it beside the other.*)

SLEEVE: And in the jar with the proper label! I don't want him remembering things before they *happen!*

NURSE: Yes, sir. (*Musingly, lowered voice.*) There's something wrong with my motor nerves today. (NURSE *busily gets patient back onto table.* PAULA, *overhearing her remark, stares at her.* NORM *picks up a rather large hand-drill.*)

SLEEVE: (*To* NORM.) Really, you're not going to use a three-quarter inch drill?!

NORM: (*Lowered voice.*) The other's broken.

NURSE: (*To* SLEEVE, *confidingly, mincingly.*) That hard-headed contractor we did last week.

SLEEVE: (*Exchanges shrugs with her.*) It's going to be hell when we re-wire his nerves again. (*Peering into skull.*) Lot of moral fiber there.

NORM: (*Coming around to other side.*) Look, J.E., I'm coming in from the front. Then I'll work up until I run into your pinking shears.

SLEEVE: Fine! (*Dryly.*) And be sure you know what you're cutting! The last time you chopped off a piece of my fingernail. (*Sound of frogs croaking as* PAULA *opens window. They glance at her, she closes it.*)

NILES: (*Dreamily; narrative voice.*) I may never know now which things I imagined, and which were real. Since the operation, people have insisted that I dreamed up the entire thing . . . doctors, nurse, power-tools and all.

NORM: (*Excitedly; he has heard.*) J.E.! Notice something?!

SLEEVE: I'm noticing!

NORM: He's ahead of us!

SLEEVE: Ahead of us! We've advanced him several weeks!

NORM: Because of the pressure! Take out your ballpoint pen and try that darning needle.

SLEEVE: (*He does. The patient reacts.*) He predicted we might have to use the electric sander!

NORM: How deep are you in there? Here. (*He produces an ordinary yardstick and hands it to* SLEEVE.)

SLEEVE: Don't you have anything smaller than that? Where's the tape-measure?

NORM: It's got blood on it.

SLEEVE: (*Shrugs, and inserts yardstick.*) Inch and five-eighths, give or take a little. Nurse! Take the hydrometer and see if my battery's up!

NURSE: (*Does.*) Yes sir. (NURSE *glances at* PAULA *who is extremely disturbed by the haphazard procedure.*)

SLEEVE: Sooner or later I'm going to have to insist that we find ourselves a set up with regular electric current.

NURSE: (*Calling to Doctor.*) One of your cells is dead. Otherwise, you're okay.

NILES: Thank you.

NURSE: Sweetie! I was talking to . . .

NILES: (*Cuts her off: vague, wandering.*) Where am I *now?* I hear music.

NURSE: It's the carnival, Chuck! Near town.

NILES: Let's go! (*Pause.*) *What* town?

NURSE: (*Evasive; a glance at doctors.*) Just a town . . . (*Pause.*) How does your head feel?

NILES: What's ahead?

NURSE: (*Comfortingly, friendly, baby talk.*) A head's the thing that sits on your neck and causes all the troub- . . .

The Reactivated Man

NILES: (*Blurts, cutting her off.*) I know that! I mean, *ahead!* The future! (*Pause; now softly.*) I feel the future.
SLEEVE: (*A glance at* NORM.) Yes . . . ?
NILES: Is it over?
NORM: What? (*As in "Is what over?"*)
NILES: (*Feebly.*) War.
NORM: (*Questioning glance at* PAULA. *She comes up toward them.*) Which war?
NILES: Any war, I guess. (*He slumps back. They manifest discouragement.*)
PAULA: (*Figuratively shaking her head in doubt.*) I don't see any change yet.
SLEEVE: (*Nodding in agreement.*) He's not *ready* yet.
NORM: (*Serene, takes a few lecturing steps.*) We've temporarily shorted out the past. You noticed the feeling of lightness upon the part of the patient? (PAULA *appears doubtful.*)
NURSE: As though an awful burden was gone! (*Pause.*) He was happy as hell for an instant!
SLEEVE: But there remain the present and future. The present, in these types, inevitably presses for the *future*. And the future remains dark until we have scraped clean the damaging tissues of collective guilt.
PAULA: But suppose—
NURSE: I know it sounds complicated, but J.E.'s right.
SLEEVE: Sometimes, just cutting out a few milligrams of *recall* does the job. Say, the patient is suffering from some unpunished personal guilt . . .
NURSE: Like child molesting! (*Notes* PAULA's *reaction.*) Or joining some . . . some subversive organization.
NILES: (*To himself.*) I . . . didn't . . . join . . . because of Paula.
NURSE: (*With quick cheer.*) That's as good a reason as any, Chuck!
NILES: (*Hasn't heard her.*) I'm guilty for *not* joining. Paula's guilty for not *letting* me.
PAULA: Charles!
NORM: Joining what?
SLEEVE: Joining what?
NORM: The Auto Club?
SLEEVE: The Auto Club?
NILES: (*He doesn't hear them. Drugged, slurred speech.*) But now . . . ever'thing's . . . going to be all right . . . all right . . . all right . . . (*Pause.*) For me, that is . . . for me . . . that is . . .

Faintly is heard a few bars of the forlorn nickelodeon theme-song music. PAULA *stiffly heads for the window: dejected, hunched, with Kleenex. Doctors freeze as a tableau. Suddenly,* PAULA *runs to window and throws it open. Instantly, loudly the "quickie" music comes on again. The doctors and* NURSE *again move quickly, jerkily under strobe light, working feverishly with power tools, etc. Then music slows to half speed and all mime in slow motion for a few beats. Then music slows distortedly like a run-down phonograph and ceases. The tableau freezes. It resumes at "quickie" speed once more and the frenzied ballet under strobe light goes on until* PAULA *marches jerkily to operating table, turns, marches back to window and closes it. This stops the music.*

Momentary blackout.

Lights come on to reveal doctors relaxed. NURSE, *with fly-swatter is creeping around floor, swatting at cockroaches.* PAULA *sits alert, tense, waiting.*

SLEEVE: (*Going over to corner, pulls out a dart game.*) That'll hold him for awhile!

NORM: That it will! (*He gets out a comic book.* SLEEVE *begins throwing darts at target. Pause.*)

PAULA: Is it . . . what happens now?

NURSE: They got to wait until the ice cubes freeze his obbligato.

PAULA: The what?

NURSE: (*Shrugs.*) I never can remember that word. (*Pause.*) Want a fix? (PAULA *shakes her head.*) Like to share a joint? (PAULA *shakes head.*) Gin? Coffee? Tea? . . . How about a burrito . . . only I can't heat it because we've got to use the gas later for the blow-torch. (NORM, *reading, bursts out laughing; he will continue to do this intermittently.* PAULA *notes this casualness with astonishment.*)

PAULA: (*Now back to* NURSE's *statement.*) Did you say . . . blow-torch?

NURSE: (*Throws up hands.*) No! You're right! I meant *soldering-iron.* (*Waits; explains.*) They have to solder his you-know later on. Otherwise—

SLEEVE: Miss Thanatopsis! Did you remember to get Plastic Wood when you were in town?

NURSE: Natch.

SLEEVE: And the thumb tacks?

NURSE: Natch. (*Pause.*) No! I remembered. But then I forgot. We've paperclips though. *Loads.* (NORM *laughs loudly again, terminating the problem.*)

The Reactivated Man

PAULA: (*Uneasily watching the two unconcerned doctors. To* NURSE.) Uh, they didn't do anything yet. Right?
NURSE: Right. J.E. always makes a few practice tries first. Every brain's a little different than different ones.
PAULA: Will he feel it . . . when they cut?
NURSE: Not like the way pain is. He'll do a lot of fighting and begging. But it won't actually hurt.
PAULA: Will he . . . Will he talk much?
NURSE: (*A shy laugh.*) You'll hear words you never dreamed that yet existed! (NORM *laughs loudly;* PAULA *realizes he is still reacting to the comic book.*)
PAULA: Will he say a lot of derogatory . . . (*She suspects* NURSE *doesn't know the word.*) a lot of unkind things about me?
NURSE: Natch! But it doesn't mean a thing! Actually, they're only arguing with themselves. It's because of this split-level personality.
PAULA: Hmmm?
NURSE: (*Laughter.*) That's what J.E. calls a schizoid. (*Pause.*) When you get in there, the unconscious is triggered and it starts a fight with the conscious. (*She pauses as both watch.* SLEEVE *brings out a badminton set.*) Damndest thing you ever heard! It sounds like two different persons coming out of the same tongue! (*Pause.*) *Three* persons! Four! Once we had a boy from Kansas that suddenly started talking Chinese! Once we had a redneck farmer that all at once thought he was a black guy on a slave ship. He . . . (*Abruptly pauses; remembering something important.*) Hey! Incidentally, you forgot to remember to fill in that part of the questionaire where it says about *"color."*
PAULA: (*Bitter; contemptuously.*) I couldn't think of a color.
NURSE: (*Surprised.*) Hmm?
PAULA: Color. True blue? Red? Yellow? (*Pause.*) He doesn't believe in fighting for his rights.
NURSE: You're putting me on.
PAULA: I was putting you off.
NURSE: (*Warm and sympathetic again.*) I don't mind. That questionaire asks a lot of personal shit. (*Pause.*) You, uh, left out a lot.
PAULA: (*Grim laugh.*) I wanted to pass him off as a square instead of a freak. I was afraid the doctors might be prejudiced . . . unsympathetic.
NURSE: (*Heartily.*) They couldn't care *less!* You pays your money

and you . . . (*She breaks off; shock registers.*) Hey! (*Lowers voice.*) I forgot to get the money from you! Norm and J.E. will—
PAULA: (*Shrugs helplessly.*) I don't—(*Pause; gestures.*) It's all in Charles' pocket. Nine hundred.
NURSE: (*Glancing at doctors and* NILES.) Wow! My memory . . .
PAULA: Shall I go over and—
NURSE: (*Cuts her off with violent head shake.*) Jesus! If they ever found out I forgot something like that—
PAULA: Don't worry about it. We'll slip it to you later.
NURSE: (*Unconvinced; wondering what to do.*) Yeah, but Chuck might . . . (*Pause.*) Sometimes they—
PAULA: (*Lays a friendship hand.*) Don't worry! Charles may be a lot of things but he's not a crook.
NURSE: (*Vague; still concerned.*) Yeah.
PAULA: That's his problem. He's *too* honest.
NURSE: Yeah.
NORM: (*To* SLEEVE; *looking up from comic book.*) Hey! Know what Linda Lovelace does with her time when she's not busy eating?
SLEEVE: Of course! (*He picks up a dart and starts throwing it at an enlarged photo of Sigmund Freud.* NORM *goes back to his reading.*)
NURSE: (*To* PAULA.) Uh . . . when did Charles begin to decide to let it all hang out?
PAULA: Mmmm?
NURSE: What I mean is, when did he start to put it all *together*. (*Pause.*) For instance, this vegetarian trip?
PAULA: (*Shrugs.*) Who knows! Who knows when something changes inside us? (*Pause.*) The fact is, Charles used to be crazy about hunting and fishing. He was an expert shot. We had deer, quail, pheasant . . . you name it! Then, one night at dinner he suddenly looked at me with a strange expression! (*Pause.*) He looked at me and said, "I heard it quack!"
NURSE: (*Puzzled.*) What?
PAULA: *Quack.*
NURSE: Quack? (*She does.*) Quack! Quack! *Quack?* (*The doctors stare at her;* NILES *stirs.*) Like a duck? (*Waits.*) Well?
PAULA: It was on the plate. (*Pause.*) Cooked. (*Pause.*) The duck.
NURSE: (*Long, long pause.*) Oh. (SLEEVE *puts darts aside, starts bouncing a badminton shuttlecock on the racquet.*)
SLEEVE: Hey? You guys want to join in? We got extra racquets. (*He playfully bats one at* NURSE. *He bats another at* PAULA, *who shakes her head but manages a civil smile.* SLEEVE *retrieves the shuttlecock and*

The Reactivated Man

bats one at NORM *who irritably swings at it with his comic book.*)
NURSE: (*Answering* PAULA's *disapproval.*) They like to relax once in awhile. It's really important *therapy!* (NORM *leaps up, seizes a racquet and savagely bats one at* SLEEVE's *head.*) I know it probably seems strange.
PAULA: Nothing seems strange any . . . (*Breaks off.*)
NORM: (*Chasing* SLEEVE *with racquet.*) Olé! (SLEEVE *darts behind* NILES. NORM *starts batting just over* NILES *head.* PAULA *registers fear.*)
NURSE: (*Admiringly.*) They *really* like to relax! (SLEEVE *and* NORM *become aware of the impression they are making and move away from* NILES. NURSE, *remembering her thoughts, confronts* PAULA.) Uh . . . why is it you didn't want Chuck to join the radical movement?
PAULA: The what? (*Now uncomfortably.*) It's a very complicated story.
NORM: (*Dancing around, batting.*) Olé!
NURSE: According to the questionaire you're from a wealthy family. (*Pause.*)
PAULA: (*Cryptically.*) A *long* way from it now!
NURSE: And Chuck was poor. And radical?
PAULA: (*Nods.*) But I was *rich* and radical. (*She gets up. Paces.*) They make the best kind! The rebellious offspring of upper middleclass families.
NURSE: (*Doubtfully.*) Yeah. Well . . . They do?
PAULA: But they get over it quickly!
NURSE: (*Suddenly disturbed and curious.*) Why?
PAULA: (*Gesture of helplessness.*) I don't know. (*Beat.*) Maybe it's some kind of unwritten tribal law. (*Beat.*) Survival of the fittest. Natural selection.
NORM: (*Again he darts precariously close to* NILES *to bat the shuttlecock.*) Olé!
SLEEVE: (*As* NORM *misses.*) Touché!
NURSE: (*Believes she understands; nods.*) Well my dad owned a laundramat. I hated every minute of it.
PAULA: (*Disturbed, watching* NORM.) Mmmm . . . (*Pause.*) You what?
NURSE: I dropped out. But then after awhile I began dropping *in* again.
SLEEVE: (*To* PAULA *and* NURSE.) Anybody for a shot of one-ninety-eight proof laboratory alcohol?

NURSE: (*Starts to respond; catches herself on seeing* PAULA. *Righteously.*) I'm *on duty!* (PAULA *shakes her head. Politely.*)
NORM: I will. With ice.
SLEEVE: Ice? We used it all. Remember?
NORM: So? (*He crosses to* NILES *and reaches inside his bandaged head as* PAULA *stares, carries cubes to sink, rinses them off, pours two drinks.*)
NURSE: (*Oblivious to* PAULA's *shock.*) I even joined the flower children. Nevertheless . . .
PAULA: Mmmmmmmm? (*Forces herself to be polite and attentive.*) Excuse me. I missed that.
NURSE: *Flower* children. Until they started ripping each other off. (*An impassioned gesture.*) Everybody's the same! Even if they *are* different! (*The teakettle is starting to whistle. She removes it. Comes back to* PAULA. *Now shyly.*) Would you like to hear my final conclusion bout *everything?*
PAULA: (*Vaguely.*) Yes. (*Now with sincere eagerness.*) Yes. I would!
NURSE: Just this! No matter where you are on the outside. When you look back inside, then turn it inside out, you're right back where you started on the outside!! (*The teakettle falls from her hand. Immediately, and for no apparent reason,* NILES *begins to hum "Yankee Doodle."*)
NORM: Nurse! (NURSE *quickly grabs kettle and starts for operating table.* NILES *goes on humming.*) No! No! Not yet! Paperclips 'll do! (NURSE *rummages through a not-clinical-looking bucket.*)
NURSE: (*Shaking head.*) How about bobby pins? (NORM *nods. She pulls two or three from her hair. Hands them to him. As he twists a turniquet around* NILES's *head, the tempo of the tune slows, much like a phonograph record running down.* SLEEVE *assists. Together, they twist until the tune stops midway.* NURSE *hands* SLEEVE *the kettle which he pours through a funnel atop* NILES's *head. There is a reaction, then stillness.* NURSE *to* PAULA.) They got to melt the ice.
PAULA: Oh.
NURSE: (*Sits with* PAULA.) Ummmmmm . . . is Charles musically inclined?
PAULA: (*Stares for a long time.*) Not if you mean "Yankee Doodle." I never heard *that* before!
NURSE: (*Nodding.*) That's what I mean! They usually sing the *opposite* kind of music they like when the ice cubes begin to melt. (*Pause.* PAULA *looks dumbfounded.*) You know? (PAULA *smiles; shakes her head.*) Chuck was a little early. Unless it melted before it should . . . (PAULA *waits.*) The *ice* . . . (PAULA *is bewildered,*

but nods her head agreeably.) I'm glad he sang "Yankee Doodle" instead of Rachmaninoff. Or Neil Diamond. He's *resisting*.

PAULA: (*Nervous glance at operating table.*) But what about . . . afterwards? (NURSE's *cup falls to floor. Again, she seems unaware until sound of impact. The doctors react to the sound.*)

NURSE: (*Picking up pieces.*) Gee!

NORM: Dr. Sleeve! The gravitational pull seems most excessive today!

SLEEVE: It's the time of the month, sir! Saturn's directly in line with Jupiter. There's a flood tide!

NORM: And a pregnant moon!

NURSE: (*To* PAULA *examining broken cup.*) Gee! (*Shrugs.*) Sometimes you — (*She breaks off, embarrassed.*)

PAULA: (*Charitably changes subject.*) Tell me more about this music thing.

NURSE: Oh sure! Take me for instance . . . I was way into Bob Dylan and Janis Joplin before I had my operation. (*She falls silent.*)

PAULA: Yes?

NURSE: (*Triumphantly.*) Now I can't stand them! *That* was *music?* (*She falls silent again.*)

PAULA: Well . . . ? What do you prefer now?

NURSE: (*Righteously.*) Lawrence Welk! Stravinsky! Burt Bacharach! (*She observes that* PAULA *seems distressed.*) You never know! *Always!* (NILES *suddenly sings the suggestive words of a current hard-rock song. Doctors leap up and tighten clamps.* NILES *is jerking to the beat; with great effort they hold him down. Again his singing grinds to a slow halt like a run-down phono record. The* NURSE *tries to smile for* PAULA's *reassurance.*) That's a good sign! Because he isn't finished yet! He'll probably be humming Strauss waltzes by the time they put him all together! (*She notes that* PAULA *is in no way reassured.*)

PAULA: (*Long pause.*) Well?

NURSE: I'm not getting through?

PAULA: You're getting through. It's just —

NURSE: (*Sees the light.*) We don't groove! You're a . . . (*Pause.*) You come from a different . . . (*Pause.*) Your family, probably . . . (*She breaks off,* PAULA *waits.*) I was spaced out. Born that way! I took the trip . . . Drugs! Flower child! Groupie . . . (*She paces.*) Whereas you . . .

PAULA: (*Long pause; quietly.*) *I* was a groupie. (NURSE *appears*

uninterested, she does not believe this.) Yes! (PAULA *now leaps up and starts to pace;* NURSE *withdraws. Impassionedly.*) Not so far back as you might think! Me! I was one of the post-pubic camp followers who yank beads and earrings off rock and roll heroes! Me — (*A low moaning from* NILES *stops her;* NURSE *glances at* PAULA *questioningly.*) There wasn't any Charles Niles then! Only a beautiful unformed boy who played bass! And I? I was just the girl next to ten thousand other girls who dwelt within that private, vacant city of the mind they call 'youth.' (*She waits for* NURSE *to absorb this.*) We thought we could put it together by letting it all hang out! With or without a bra.
NURSE: (*Surprised, but laughs.*) That's good! Because you can laugh —
PAULA: (*With unexpected fury.*) It was excruciating! They were Gods . . . up there on that platform! Wild! Unattainable! Trampling all the rules! And all that unleashed electronic power . . . that unerring beat that shook your glands. (*The doctors are fascinated; they move towards her.* NILES *stirs.* NURSE *is bewitched.*) It turned you into jelly . . . and a million vaginas opened and waited! No . . . begged! Mine was one of them. (*Aware that she's becomes a spectacle,* PAULA *hesitates.*)
NURSE: Go on!
PAULA: (*More down to earth.*) It was the Children's Crusade, 1960. The bloodless revolution! We were out to overthrow order, discipline, responsibility! Work became a dirty word! Success was obscene! (*Rising crescendo.*) All you had to do was *be* . . . *be* there . . . drowned in the mass hysteria of failure worship!
NURSE: But it wasn't failure! It was hero worship! The guys up there on the bandstand —
PAULA: (*In fury*) And why! Because God was permissive! Indulgent! You didn't have to comb your hair! Wash your clothes! You could slurp coca cola and pop bubblegum! No dishes to wash! No chores! No rules! All the pleasures and privileges of being grown up without the work of getting there. (*The doctors have become so entranced that they're unaware of* NILES's *writhing.*) Why! Why? Because some adolescent oracle came up with the marvelous idea that you could create your hero in your own image and likeness! Father and Mother were past thirty! Bourgeois!
NURSE: They were what?
PAULA: Square. No communication! The truth was to come from freaks in soiled leather pants . . . babbling in monosyllables.

(NURSE, *aware of* NILES's *distress, glances at doctors. They hurry over and start to administer.* PAULA *somewhat purged, and embarrassed, tries to force a laugh. Now in lower tones.*) Well. (*Pause.*) That's about it.

NURSE: Please! You were going to tell me what happened.

PAULA: (*Almost to herself.*) Yes. I was, wasn't I?

NURSE: Why you stopped. Being a groupie . . .

PAULA: (*Reluctantly, from deep within.*) Oh, seven years is a long time! (*Suddenly recharged.*) I'll *tell* you what happened! It happened at Woodstock! There was this boy that played . . . bass? With his hair in a pony tail, and standard dark glasses and fuzz, so all you saw was his mouth, which was exactly like Peter Fonda's. (NURSE *sits, but on edge of chair.*) Grim and curled. Sneering at all the falseness of the world. Later . . . well, later . . .

NURSE: Well, what's wrong with sneering at the falseness of the world?

PAULA: It had nothing to do with the falseness of the world!

NURSE: (*Gets up, glancing nervously toward doctors.*) So what happened?

PAULA: I'm trying to tell you what happened! I followed this boy around Woodstock! Even Santa Ana, California. I think he even recognized me once or twice . . . Of course, with those black glasses you can't tell. They all might be looking straight at you . . . or everybody, for that matter. But something jolted me. I felt God looking straight through me and liking what he saw. I promptly soiled my underpants.

NURSE: (*A wild laugh. Then cuts her laugh quickly on seeing* NORM's *glance.*) Go on. (*Waits.*) At least it shows you had feelings. (PAULA *reacts.*) So what happened?

PAULA: (*Gets up, slowly walks toward window; alone, voice rising.*) The guitar player was screaming into the microphones, and gyrating, trying to make his pants fall down still farther. And the bass and treble were coming out at a volume you wouldn't believe . . . and everybody on the platform was caught up in a crescendo! Where it all *was!* And the multitudes on the grass . . . or on grass . . . or both . . . or acid . . . the world was united . . . moving as one . . . led by the mad Gods right over the cliff! We'd 've gone anywhere with them. (*She stops; tense, abstract.*)

NURSE: (*Caught up.*) Well? Well?

PAULA: Somebody pulled the plug. (*She starts to laugh; the sound is angry, wicked.*)
NURSE: Did what?
NORM: Nurse! (*She leaps up but cannot move until she hears the rest.*)
PAULA: Some weirdo had climbed up on the back of the stage and disconnected the amplifiers. (*She is almost screaming with rage.*) You know what happened?! You want to know what happened when all that phallic power went dead? You saw a group of pallid, pockmarked anemic little boy freaks! The guitar was a shrieking mouse! The guitar sounded like a goddamned toy ukelele! You couldn't even hear the bass player! (*She pauses.* NURSE *wildly gestures her to continue.*) They stopped. (*Pause.*) A piteous band of unkempt, pallid, insecure, dull, third rate —
NORM: (*Interrupts with a bellow.*) Nurse! (*And the nurse jumps.*)
PAULA: The bottom dropped out of the world. I saw myself, mirrored back — (NURSE *lingers now, overwhelmed.*)
SLEEVE: *Nurse!*
NURSE: (*Starts toward doctors; stops, in whisper.*) Uh . . . don't forget to remind me not to forget! The money! (*Lights dim. Carnival music; sound of marsh birds and crickets.*)
NILES: (*Again, poetic recitation.*) And so, at last, the patient was pronounced ready. He had heard the strange dialogue between wife and nurse, watching anger take on the smell of fear. And the fear? It rode nurse's shoulders to the operating table where suddenly it leaped into the doctor's eyes. I stared it down: and the odor and the sound . . . but not with the ordinary senses. For it entered me through the top of the skull, assailing my exposed nerves of precognition.
NORM: (*Humourously.*) I'm starting the countdown, J.E. Lights! Action! (NURSE *pushes lantern to patient's head.*)
SLEEVE: Sooner the better! He's ahead of us again.
NORM: Practically into tomorrow! Bombs away!
NILES: (*Disclaiming poetically.*) It was all very good-humored. (*Pause.*) Later it would prove to be even more humorous.
SLEEVE: (*Watches* NORM *hover uncertainly over patient with icepick. The sight still revolts him. He lights a cigarette and walks to window, looks out, waiting.*) Well, Doc?
NORM: Well?
SLEEVE: *Well?*
NORM: (*Demanding, angry.*) Well?
SLEEVE: (*Furious.*) *Well?*

The Reactivated Man

NILES: (*Declaiming, poetically.*) Still he hesitated. He seemed to listen for the pounding sea a quarter mile away across windswept dunes. Then, sliding his Phi Beta Kappa key into his rear pocket — presumably so it wouldn't see what he was about to do — he turned on me with unleashed vigor! (*In silhouette against the rear walls we see the icepick plunge downward to patient's skull.* NILES *emits a bloodcurdling scream.* PAULA *leaps up.*)

NURSE: (*Tense, but game.*) Hold tight, darling! (NORM *plunges instrument again, patient screams again, but less urgently.* PAULA *back to audience, appears to vomit.* NURSE *sees this but remains at her post.*)

SLEEVE: (*Joyously.*) Bull's-eye, doctor!

NORM: *Two!* But it'll take more!!! (*Plunges icepick again. This time, patient's cry is a whimper.* NORM *starts to plunge again.* NILES *tries to move his head out of the way.*)

NILES: (*In a new, strange voice which will occur intermittently henceforth, the so-called Inner Voice of his subconscious which will now be in a stage whisper.*) Please! Gentlemen! I've never hurt *you!* I've never hurt anyone!

NORM: It's still alive. Take your screwdriver and push! No . . . more to the right! (SLEEVE *pushes screwdriver.*)

NILES: (*Inner voice.*) No! Other way!

NORM: (*Scoldingly.*) I said '*to the right.*' Not *left* —

SLEEVE: I *am* pushing to the right! Don't you know right from left?

NORM: Don't you? (*Holds up hand.*) This is my right hand! (*Holds up other hand.*) This is my *left* hand! (PAULA *listens with agitation;* NURSE *is used to this, but is concerned for* PAULA.)

SLEEVE: (*Imitates gestures of* NORM.) So? And this is *my* right hand! And this is my *left* hand! So if you tell me to push the goddamned screwdriver to the right, I push this way. (*He demonstrates.* NILES *moans.* PAULA *rushes toward them but stops helplessly.*)

NURSE: Wait! Norm! He's right! I mean *left!* I mean . . . (*She breaks off, addresses* PAULA.) The whole problem's simple! One of the doctors is *backwards!*

SLEEVE: (*Outraged.*) *Who* is?

NORM: (*Outraged.*) *Who* is?

NURSE: I mean —

PAULA: (*Furiously, uncontrolled.*) You're *facing* each other! Right for one is wrong for the other! I mean —

NURSE: She means *left.* If one says 'push to the right,' it means the other one's left! (*The doctors think this over in exasperated confusion.* PAULA *waits tensely. A long pause.*)

NILES: (*Cheerily.*) Boop! Boop! A Doop!! (*All astonishedly face him.*)
PAULA: (*Horrified.*) Charles!!
NILES: Boop-boop-a-doop!
NURSE: (*As doctors go into action, zestfully.*) He's in Outer Space already! Left was right after all!
NORM: Harder, J.E.!
SLEEVE: (*Twists,* NURSE *smiles.*) It just doesn't want to die!
NILES: (*Inner Voice.*) Kill me then! Go ahead! Try!
NILES: (*Calmly.*) The nurse's face smiled. She was unable to feel pain vicariously.
NORM: (*Calling.*) Charles Niles! Can you hear me?
NILES: (*Calmly.*) Which Charles Niles are you calling?
NORM: The other one! (*To* SLEEVE.) I think we've got it, J.E. Really I do.
SLEEVE: Nurse! The patient's Behavioral pattern —
NURSE: But he has no pattern, remember?
NORM: He had one in '45.
NURSE: It was removed in June, '46.
NORM: The fools! Didn't they replace it with anything?
NURSE: This cat's a stylist! He invents his pattern after the fact!
NILES: I would have laughed, but they had clamped my Sense of Humor onto my subconscious. All I could do was cry a little while they stood there, swinging their keys and storing up resentments.
SLEEVE: (*Probing with screw driver.*)
NILES: Mmmmmmmm?
SLEEVE: Why haven't you supported your wife and family in the customary manner?
NILES: (*Inner Voice.*) Can't afford it. (*The* NURSE *angles around to see if she can get to his pants pocket for the money.*)
SLEEVE: You've a college degree in engineering? Why'd you leave a lucrative profession?
NURSE: (*Confidingly.*) There are certain things not shown in the case history.
NORM: (*Sarcastic.*) Imagine that, Dr. Sleeve!
NURSE: He quit a position with the government. Because it was *war work.*
NORM: (*Stops work.*) He what?
NILES: (*Inner Voice.*) *Missiles.* I got to thinking I was digging my own grave.
NURSE: He don't kill ducks or anything! Do you, Charles?

NORM: (*Sternly.*) Nurse! Don't coach the patient!
SLEEVE: You've got to be realistic, Mr. Niles! You've got to think of your wife and children.
NILES: (*Inner Voice.*) That's why I'm here.
NORM: J.E.! *Harder!* (SLEEVE *thrusts.*)
NILES: (*Inner Voice. Weak, gasping.*) Please! I mustn't die! (*Active Voice; harshly.*) You've *got* to! (*Inner Voice.*) You'll turn into a monster! The other half is always a monster. (*Active Voice; tautly.*) Shut up. Please.
PAULA: (*Anguishedly, lays hand on* SLEEVE.) Doctor! (*They stand back, irritated.*)
NURSE: He's doing just great, Paula!
PAULA: Are you sure? (*Pause.*) Are you sure it's all right?
NORM: (*Humorously.*) I've never lost a soul yet!
NILES: (*Active Voice; he jerks up.*) That's why I'm *here! To lose my soul!*
SLEEVE: (*Gesturing* NURSE *to get him down again.*) Nurse!
NURSE: (*Coaxing him back.*) Not your *soul!* It's just a little old pimple the size of a flea!
SLEEVE: *Unnatural growth!*
NURSE: Like leprosy or anything.
NORM: (*To* PAULA.) The soul will be left absolutely intact.
SLEEVE: Just like anybody else's.
NILES: (*Inner Voice.*) But he doesn't *want* a soul just like anybody else's!
NORM: (*In a fury.*) Oh? (*He applies a mechanic's wrench.* NILES *screams anew.*)
NURSE: (*To* PAULA *and all with hearty cheer.*) His *scream* is coming through just swell!
SLEEVE: (*Modestly.*) A bit strident! Left syndrome is severed, but—
NORM: (*Cuts in peevishly.*) Quickly now, J.E.!! Before it has time to recover! Nurse! (*She brings to* SLEEVE *an electronic-looking complex of wires and two chrome rods, attached by wires to a box.* SLEEVE *reaches into skull with the two probers, fixes them, waits. To* NILES.) Say something.
NILES: (*Hopefully.*) Mother?
NORM: (*Nods at* SLEEVE, *who tries a new position with the nodes.*) Go on! Anything!
NILES: (*Chants these words off precisely, loudly.*) Anything. Of. think. Can't. Boom.
NURSE: He's coming through backwards.
NILES: (*High, Germanic proclamation.*) Ach!

NORM: (*To* PAULA.) He was stationed in Germany during the Occupation?
PAULA: (*Shakes her head.*) He wasn't in the war. Conscientious objector. (*Pause.*) He speaks no foreign languages. (SLEEVE *probes again with the mechanism.*)
NILES: Forgive them for they know not what they do. (*All glance at one another.* PAULA *shrugs.* SLEEVE *tries again.*)
NORM: Mr. Niles, is there something important you would like to tell us?
NILES: (*Quickly.*) Mary had a little lamb. (NORM *gestures for* SLEEVE *to try another position. He does.*)
NILES: (*Impassionedly, almost pleading and sobbing.*) Mary! Mary! Mary! (SLEEVE *quickly moves the nodes.*)
PAULA: Charles!
NILES: (*Now cheerily and sing-song.*) Mary had a little. Mary had a little. Mary had a little. Mary had a—(SLEEVE *reaches around and tries nodes on another part of brain.*)
NILES: (*Conversationally.*) Why not, Alice? Isabelle? Barbara? Lucille?
NORM: (*Cuts him off. Sees* PAULA's *concern.*) You're fumbling, J.E.! Fumbling! (SLEEVE *goes around to other side of table and tries again.*)
NILES: (*Declaration, but as though surprised.*) I went limp on the courthouse steps! I went limp on the courthouse steps! I went . . . (SLEEVE *tries again.* NILES *continues in marchtime.*) Limp. Limp. Limp. Li- . . . (SLEEVE *tries again.*) Mary had a little limp.
NORM: J.E.! Damn you, J.E.! (SLEEVE *with exasperated look at* NORM, *tries again. Gets down on knees for better position.*)
NILES: (*In Castilian tongue.*) Ghandi! Es un pacifisto, no? (*Pause; dramatically.*)This above all, to thine own self . . . (SLEEVE *tries again. Laughingly.*) Mary tried non-violent resistance on me! (*Laughs. He continues laughing until* SLEEVE *removes the nodes.*)
NORM: (*Irritated, demandingly of* SLEEVE.) What *is* all this *drivel* you're getting me?
NURSE: But it makes sense! It's all part of his beliefs!
NILES: (*Without being probed.*) Megatons.
NORM: (*Leans over him.*) Yes?
NILES: They're not quite ready to take their place . . . megatons. (NORM *seizes the hydrometer. He aims it at* NILE's *brain, but waits.* NILES *sings to tune of "Over There."*) Ov-er-kill! Over-kill! Over-kill . . . over-kill . . . over—(NORM *squirts liquid from hydro-*

The Reactivated Man

meter on NILE's *head as though extinguishing a fire. Thoughtfully, after a pause.*) They turned the fire hoses on us in Mississippi.
NORM: They what?
SLEEVE: They what?
NILES: Fire hoses.
NORM: (*Humoring him.*) Oh. (*Doctors glance at each other as if patient is crazy.*)
SLEEVE: (*Humoring him.*) Oh.
NORM: (*Whispers.*) This will never do!
SLEEVE: Never!
NORM: Never!
SLEEVE: Never!
NORM: Never! (*Now with anger.*) You got his *responses* all fucked up!
SLEEVE: (*Angry.*) Oh I have, have I?
NORM: (*Snaps pinking shears dangerously.*) I knew it from the time he went "boom!"
SLEEVE: He what?
NILES: Boom! (NORM *resignedly picks up electric drill, turns it off and on.* NURSE, *anticpating that he is about to rectify a mistake wrongly diagnosed, puts hand on him.*)
NURSE: Wait! Please! Sir! Stop! He's coming through perfectly okay! The fire hoses . . .
PAULA: It's true! He was in the civil rights march down south! They used fire hoses to break it up. (*The doctors think this over.*)
NILES: (*As though lecturing.*) Peace begins and ends with the little things . . . such as not honking your horn, or killing the umpire. (*The doctors shrug this off, glancing at the two women, who nod understandingly.*) Peace is equality! Honesty! Justice!
NORM: (*Dryly.*) Brilliant deduction, J.E.!
SLEEVE: An amazing concept! Amazing! We've raised his I.Q. to 69.
NORM: Higher! I'd say 74!
NILES: (*Inner Voice.*) The problem is to love your neighbor.
SLEEVE: *Astounding!* I never thought of that! Did you, doctor?
NORM: *Never!* Did you?
SLEEVE: Never! How about you?
NORM: Never! What about you?
SLEEVE: Never! And you?
NORM: Never! Besides . . . I don't have any neighbors. Do you?
SLEEVE: Not I! Have you got neighbors?
NORM: No. Have you?

SLEEVE: No.
NILES: (*Inner Voice.*) Whole world is neighbor.
SLEEVE: Think of that!
NORM: I *am* thinking! Does he mean Japs, Wops, Democrats, Kikes, Krauts, Spics and Frogs?
SLEEVE: Or Commies, Greasers, Niggers, Rednecks, Southern Californians, Cops, Dagos, Seventh Day Adventists, or Hippies?
NORM: What about China? Russia? Cuba?
NILES: (*Inner Voice, but excitedly.*) Si! Es verdad!! (*He switches to Russian, German, French, Chinese.*)
NORM: (*Distressed.*) Goddamn it, J.E.! You've caused him to defect! (*Quickly the doctors bring out new power tools and gadgets. They twist and probe; then wait.*)
NILES: (*A new, fatherly, authoritative voice.*) Of course, one has to be practical about these things! Just because some half-baked religious zealot got goosed by a hippopotamus and . . .
PAULA: (*Screams.*) Charles! (*All glance at each other in astonishment. Smiles of triumph begin to register upon the faces of the doctors.* NURSE *is joyous until she sees* PAULA's *concern.*)
SLEEVE: (*Taking out a pencil and pad and taking a stance as though interviewing* NILES.) Care to add anything to that statement, sir?
NILES: (*Same new voice.*) Definitely! Go take a flying fuck at the moon! (PAULA *fights tears.*)
NORM: (*Utterly pleased and delighted.*) Well!
SLEEVE: Well!
NURSE: (*Radiantly.*) That's telling 'em, Chuck! (*Now to* PAULA *more subdued, apologetic.*) He's right in the groove! You *got* to be practical! (NURSE *drops pliers.*)
NILES: (*New Voice.*) Practical! (*Inner Voice.*) But loving your neighbor *is* practical. (*Doctors register disappointment. New Voice, like doctors'.*) Oh? (*Inner Voice.*) That time has come when it is cheaper to help your neighbors than to defend yourself against them. (*New Voice.*) That's some platitude, Charley!! Wow!!!
SLEEVE: Wow!!!
NORM: Wow!!!
NURSE: Wow!!! (*Aside to* PAULA.) Actually, I'm just kidding him along.
NILES: (*Inner Voice.*) Snap. Drap. Clapp. Bapp. Sap. Whap. Nap. (*Pause.*) Sleep. Creep. Deep. Beep. Gleep. (*Doctors make rapid adjustments with instruments.*) Coo coo! Poopoo!

The Reactivated Man

NURSE: (*Turning back sheets; joyously.*) He's soiled his trousers already! Usually it takes *ages!*
NILES: (*Inner Voice.*) Hiss. Piss. Bliss. Kiss.
SLEEVE: (*Making adjustments.*) I don't want you free-associating yet, Mr. Niles.
NORM: (*Making adjustments.*) I don't want you free-associating yet, Mr. Niles.
NILES: (*New Voice.*) I don't want you free associating yet, Mr. Niles. (*Inner Voice.*) Wow! (*New Voice.*) *Wow!* (*Pause.*) Now! What's this threadbare old platitude about turning the other cheek? (*Pause. Inner Voice.*) Well, uh . . . (*Doctors and* NURSE *react excitedly to his hesitation. New Voice.*) All right, Niles. Come clean! (*Inner Voice.*) I . . .
NURSE: (*Cheerleaderlike.*) Come on, Chuck! Tell it to yourself like it is! (*Pause. She drops something.*) I mean "isn't." (*Pause.*) I mean is! (*Pause. They tensely wait.*)
NILES: (*Inner Voice.*) Why are you always dropping things or knocking something over? (NURSE *is stymied.* PAULA *glances questioningly at her. Doctors also react.* SLEEVE *knocks over a test tube.* NORM *drops his saw.*)
SLEEVE: (*Singsong.*) Charley! You're evading! *Evading!*
NILES: (*New Voice.*) Charley! You're evading! *Evading!* What about *peace?* Would you be peaceful if somebody tried to rape your wife? (*The three of them, encouraged by* NILES's *New Voice, wait with renewed hope. Inner Voice.*) I . . . (*Pause.*) Uh . . . (*Long pause.*)
SLEEVE: A *foreign* person!
NORM: Of questionable color!
NILES: (*Instantly; subconscious.*) I'd let him! (PAULA *winces. Doctors are outraged.* NURSE *shakes her head sadly. Suddenly, mysteriously, the windows fly open, flooding the room, loudly, with the theme music.* NILES *leaps from operating table.*)
NILES: (*New Voice; shouting above music.*) No! No! Like hell you would!
SLEEVE: (*Wildly; trying to hear.*) Nurse! close that window!
NORM: (*Calling.*) We've told you a thousand times . . .
NURSE: (*Rushing to window.*) I didn't open it!!!
PAULA: It was the wind!
SLEEVE: There *is* no wind!
NURSE: It won't close! (*Doctors agitatedly react, wanting to go and get window closed, but afraid to disturb instruments attached to* NILES's *head. Music continues to play at full volume.*)

SLEEVE: (*Shouting.*) Charles Niles! What were you telling yourself?
NORM: (*Shouting.*) About somebody raping your wife? (*Music stops as suddenly as it began; all glance toward windows.*)
NILES: (*New Voice.*) I'd beat the shit out of them. (*Music comes on; a fast, cheery beat of the nickelodeon tunes.*)
NORM: (*wildly.*) He's got it!
SLEEVE: (*Wildly.*) Freeze him right there!

NURSE *races to shelves, returns with what appears to be a spray can. Doctors excitedly aim it at* NILES's *head and set adjustments.* NURSE *does a few steps of whatever is currently called dancing.* PAULA *stares out window. Blackout.*

NILES: (*In the darkness. Subconscious; poetic recall.*) The newly awakened man . . . completely renovated and prefabricated . . . is aware first of a new girl.
NURSE: Come on, sweetie! Try!
NILES: And then, an old wife.
PAULA: Charles! Stop acting so silly! (*Lights come up. The doctors are smoking.* NILES *is propped up and reaching for a cigarette that* NURSE *holds out. But his hand keeps missing; it won't go where it should.*)
NURSE: (*Cheerily, to* PAULA.) Wow! He almost got it that time!
NILES: (*Poetic recall.*) They were trying to make me put it all together . . . but the birds of the marsh were gone, and the salt from the sea . . . And the music was gone . . . (*Pause.*) Something was gone . . . (NURSE *finally takes cigarette and shoves it between his lips.*)
NURSE: (*To* PAULA, *forced casualness.*) Sometimes it takes a little *longer* than sometimes. (*To* NILES.) Inhale! (NILES *unintentionally bites her finger; she screams.*)
NORM: (*Angrily throws down his cigarette.*) Shit!
SLEEVE: (*Whispers to* NORM.) Left side's still shorted out.
NORM: Right!
SLEEVE: Left!
NORM: Right!
SLEEVE: Left!
NORM: Right! (*The tempo of their argument becomes a beat, as though marching. This continues as* NILES *sings.*)
NILES: (*Hums and then sings.*) Tramp! Tramp! Tramp! The boys are marching . . . (*Angrily,* SLEEVE *reaches out and jerks the wires from* NILES's *head, 'disconnecting' him. His song winds down like a defective phonograph.* PAULA *is up, hovering worriedly.*)

NURSE: (*Cheering; consoling.*) Actually, it don't matter right now whether he leans left or right.
PAULA: But that's not—
NURSE: Right! What's important is they've completely disconnected the *Radical Middle!*
SLEEVE: (*Shouting, to cut off* NURSE.) Mr. Niles! Try your other hand!
NILES: (*Vaguely.*) Don't have any other hands.
PAULA: (*Minor wail.*) Charles! Doctor! (SLEEVE *picks up his arm, holds it straight out. It remains there. He moves it to several different positions. Each time, it remains stationary.*)
SLEEVE: Charley, move your arm. (NILES *does. With sudden, surprising force his stiff arm whacks* NORM *almost knocking him over.* PAULA *stares aghast.*)
NURSE: (*Quickly.*) He's resisting!
SLEEVE: (*Staring, happy recognition suddenly shows on his face.*) Violently!
PAULA: (*Amazement.*) Charles! (*To* NORM.) It's the first time he's ever done a thing like that! (*Pause.*) I'm sorry! He's . . . not himself!
NORM: (*Ruffled, but dignified.*) On the contrary, Mrs. Niles!!
SLEEVE: (*Excitedly.*) He *is* himself! (*Pause.*) Charley . . . (*He raises the other arm.*)
NORM: (*Demandingly.*) Niles, do you still love Reds? (NILES *wallops again. All scramble out of the way. He wallops again without help.* NORM *takes a stance, folds his arms, looks triumphantly at* PAULA.)
NURSE: (*A sly sideways glance at* PAULA.) Chuck! What do you think about guys that freaked out of the war by hiding in Canada? (NILES *gropes around, grabs a handful of instruments from the table and flings them across the room, seemingly at* PAULA.) Well!
SLEEVE: Well!
NORM: Well!
PAULA: Well!
NURSE: He wasn't aiming at you! His coordination—
NORM: Isn't very good.
SLEEVE: *Yet.*
NURSE: Remember?
NORM: (*Sidles up to* NILES. *Coyly.*) Mr. Niles! When was it you said you were going to join the American Nazi Party? (*They wait for a violent response which never comes. Slowly,* NILES's *right arm stiffens*

and he begins what apparently will become the Nazi salute; PAULA registers horror. The other three have an "I-told-you-so" expression. But the arm gets only half way to position and stops.)
SLEEVE: (*To break the deadlock.*) Charlie! Answer me, true or false! Ralph Nader would be a better President than Cesar Chavez. (*Pause.*) Unless Fidel Castro was permitted to run. (NILES *furiously throws things at* PAULA *again.*)
PAULA: Charles! It's me . . . Paula! (NILES *hears; stops. Then starts throwing things as fast as he can. She darts all over the room, dodging.*)
NORM: (*Admiringly.*) Look at that!
SLEEVE: Look at that!
NURSE: Look at that! He's actually *upset!*
SLEEVE: (*Laughs.*) Over-compensating. They always do.
NORM: They always do. (*Pause.*) Over-compensate.
NURSE: (*Nodding agreement. To* PAULA.) Always they over-compensate. Over and over. Always and always —
SLEEVE: Over and over —
NORM: Always and always.
NURSE: (*To* PAULA.) It's because they haven't replaced his memory yet. (*Pause.*) Actually, he's forgotten —
SLEEVE: To remember —
NORM: Who you *are*, Mrs. Charles.
NURSE: (*Correctively.*) Giles. (PAULA'*s expression tells her she's wrong.*) Riles. (PAULA *firms up her displeasure.*)
SLEEVE: *Lyles.* (PAULA *almost sadistically shaking head.*)
NORM: (*Sightly worried.*) Pyle? (PAULA *shakes head.*)
NURSE: Argyle? (PAULA *continues to shake head; it becomes a fascinating guessing game for the three.*)
SLEEVE: Carlisle? (PAULA *shakes head. Long pause.*)
NORM: (*Explorative.*) Smith?
NURSE: (*Trimphantly.*) Jones?
SLEEVE: *Brown?*
NORM: *White!* That's it . . . Mrs. Roger White! (*To* SLEEVE.) Eh, George?
SLEEVE: I'm Sleeve.
NORM: (*Dismissive.*) Sleeve! George! All the same thing. (*A wink to* PAULA.) Right Mrs. George? Names are a funny thing! (*He playfully buzzes the power saw near* NILES'*s cheek.*) Right Mr. Charles?
NILES: Igloo. (*The three hear this with disappointment.*)
SLEEVE: (*Comes over threateningly.*) Care to repeat that statement, sir?

The Reactivated Man

NILES: Igloo.
NURSE: (*Inspirationally.*) He's free associating again! Wow! He's trying to tell us!! These little icecubes sitting there next to his libido are cold!! (*To* PAULA.) Get it? Ice! Eskimos! *Igloo!* (To NILES.) Right, George?
NILES: I'm *Norm*.
NURSE: (*Inspirationally; to* PAULA's *concern.*) *Norm!* See what I mean! Free-associating again!
SLEEVE: Wants to be part of the *norm!*
NURSE: Like Norm! And Dr. Sleeve! (*Pause.*) Like *everybody!*
NILES: Igloo.
NURSE: (*To doctors; concerned.*) Should I . . . ?
SLEEVE: Remove the . . .
NORM: Ice? Not until . . . (*He moves to the control panel and touches knobs and buttons, watching and expecting physical reactions from the patient. He pushes a button;* NILES, *with electrode wires attached, leaps from chair.* NORM *pushes another button;* NILES *walks toward* NURSE. *He pushes another button;* NILES *stops. He pushes more buttons causing* NILES *to turn, stop, move, jump, sit, rise, walk.* PAULA *watches; winces.* NURSE *admires.* NORM *leaves control panel with* NILES *standing in middle of room and whispers to* SLEEVE; NILES *suddenly "starts up" by himself and heads for the* NURSE, *a curious look of lust on his face.*)
SLEEVE: (*Seeing* PAULA's *consternation.*) Hmmmmmmmmmmm!
NORM: *Hmmmmmmmm!* (*He leans over, pushes a button on the control.* NILES *is abruptly halted. Now with various button tunings, he makes him walk toward* PAULA. NILES *balks.* NORM *doubles the charge, jolting* NILES *forward. Finally,* NILES *stands before* PAULA *robot-like; remote.*)
SLEEVE: (*A shout; to alleviate delicate impasse.*) Charles Niles!
NORM: Charles Niles!
NORM AND SLEEVE: What are you going to do when you wake up?!
NILES: (*New voice; a hard stare at* PAULA.) What else? *Make money!*
SLEEVE: (*Pleased; but feigning skepticism.*) Oh?
NORM: (*Same.*) Oh?
NORM AND SLEEVE: And just how, may one ask, do you propose to do this?
NILES: (*Same hard stare at* PAULA.) Steal. Cheat. Rob. Mug. Murder.
PAULA: (*Her first indicative show of real anger.*) Don't look at me like that! I'd *never*—

NURSE: (*Quickly; cheerily.*) It's okay! He's *role-playing.!* (*Seductively to* NILES.) Aren't you, Charley? (NILES *responds to voice but stands threateningly.*) Tell her you're sorry, Chuck! Apologize! (NILES *remains immobile.*)
NORM: (*Fatherly; encouragingly.*) Charley . . .
SLEEVE: (*Same.*) We're all waiting, Charley. (*Long impasse.*)
PAULA: (*To all; demanding.*) Well? ? (*With a whispered oath,* NORM *steps to control panel and pushes buttons. He is trying to make* NILES *get down on his knees before* PAULA. *There becomes a Herculean struggle as* NILES *fights against bowing.* NORM, *grim and cruel, applies more electronic volume.* NILES *shudders, struggles, but each time is bent closer to the floor. Finally he is on his knees.*)
NURSE: (*Relieved, shaken. Forced cheer.*) There!
PAULA: (*Leaps up.*) This is disgusting!
NURSE: (*To* NILES; *feigns admiration.*) I *knew* you could do it if you tried, Chuck!
SLEEVE: (*Magnificently, to all.*) There's a man with a mind of his own! Bet we gave him 700 volts of electricit— (*He is cut off. A huge crash of thunder; lightning illuminates the outside window. All are visibly impressed. There is momentary silence.*)
NURSE: (*With uneasy humor.*) More than that! (*They laugh nervously.* NILES *struggles to get to his feet.*)
SLEEVE: (*In admiration.*) And still resisting.
PAULA: (*Angrily.*) Charles! Get up! You . . . you're . . .
SLEEVE: (*Aside to* NORM, *but meant for all ears.*) See what I mean, doctor?! *Resistance!* He defies even the person he most loves! (*Pause, now intimately.*) Niles . . .
NORM: Niles . . .
SLEEVE: (SLEEVE *works with the controls so that* NILES *stands; he causes* NILES *to turn around facing them.*) Niles . . . exactly what are you going to do when you walk out of here? (*Pause.*)
NORM: A completely—
SLEEVE: Beautifully—
NORM AND SLEEVE: Reactivated—
NORM: Once again able to be of use—
SLEEVE: To the society in which he dwells! (*A long wait.* SLEEVE *rapidly begins pushing the button that controls* NILES.)
NILES: (*Suddenly, rapidly.*) Yes-yes-yes-no-yes-yes-no-yes-yes yes-yes-yes—(*Another crash of thunder; the mystique has an effect on them again, but they profess to ignore it.*)
NORM: (*Chuckling.*) Going to join the Yacht Club tomorrow, Charley?

NILES: (*Shakes head.*) *Golf* club. (*Pause.*) And the Ku Klux Klan.
PAULA: (*Concerned at this last.*) Doctor!
NURSE: (*Trying unobtrusively to get* NILES'S *wallet from his trousers.*) It's all right! They always overdo when you first remove the pressure of moral behavior.
NILES: (*He grabs at* NURSE. *In a new, liberated, brash voice.*) You can say that again, sexpot! Come here! (*She eludes him.*)
NORM: (*Suavely; confident.*) Naturally, the first symptoms are *super* elation.
SLEEVE: They got to make up for lost time. (*He notes the lustful manner in* NILES'S *action.*) At the moment, patient has an elongated pithecanthropus erectus. (NURSE *emits an embarrassed giggle;* NILES *eyes doctors with reproach.*)
PAULA: A what?
NURSE: (*Cheerily.*) And it's all kind of wonderful! (*Pause.*) You . . . you feel like everything belongs to you.
NORM: (*Heartily.*) And if it don't, you grab it anyway! (*Pauses; realizes this is wrong approach.*) Of course, when we put back the rest of the recycled parts, he'll calm down a little.
NURSE: They sandpaper the Recall just enough so that patient's memories are worn off.
SLEEVE: And we shellac the ego so that—
PAULA: You do what?
NORM: The *ego.* We coat it so that it can never again be tarnished by creeping morality.
NILES: (*Deftly, he has caught* NURSE'S *arm; lowered voice.*) Look, Mata Hari . . . let's trip out! There's a carnival . . .
NURSE: (*Embarrassed; drops scissors; winks at* PAULA.) Not just now! There's work to do.
NILES: (*Aware of* PAULA'S *angered disapproval. Lowered voice.*) Who's the Mother-Figure that keeps scowling? (*A flash of lightning illuminates the faces of doctors; they are shaking their heads and reveal failure.*)
NORM: (*Coughs; clears throat; with tired dismissal.*) Well, J.E., might as well button him up. Might we?
SLEEVE: (*Same paternalistic tone.*) That we might! I see no . . .
PAULA: (*Agitatedly.*) But wait! . . . But . . .
NORM: (*Not heeding her.*) Nor do *I!* I can conscientiously declare that the patient's Homo-Intellectus has successfully undergone a cortex transplant with almost no oraculear cerebellum! Even the *Unicus-Pavlov* is allegro non troppo . . . cum laud . . . give or take an erg or two!

NURSE: (*Really overjoyed.*) Wow! I hear you! Wow!!
SLEEVE: Wow!
NILES: (*A bewildered monotone.*) Wow.

Blackout. Then, a peal of thunder and total brilliance illuminates them momentarily in fixed tableau. The blackout then resumes; now is heard the plaintive nickelodeon theme song, faintly.

NILES: (*Poetic recall.*) And so, long after they had taken me apart, they were finally putting me back together again. It all seemed like a year made up of slowly churning moments . . . (*Pause.*) Eventually, the nurse went over to the mantel and picked up my past. Neatly sanded, of course, so that the sharp edges wouldn't hurt when they put it back. And now, again, I heard a lot of people talking about things that never mattered. (*Lights up.*)
NORM: Hydrometer working properly?
NURSE: Properly, doctor.
NORM: And the spark plugs?
NURSE: Filthy. Absolutely filthy.
SLEEVE: Use much oil?
NURSE: By the quart, no less.
NILES: (*Narrator's voice.*) With relief, I realized they were talking about the nurse's used car. There was a kind of small earthquake inside me when they gave me back my ego, but I didn't actually mind. They had skillfully removed that part of me which used to fear earthquakes. (NURSE *goes back and sits at table with* PAULA.)
NORM: Well, J.E., we'd better run one last test.
SLEEVE: One last test.
NORM: Right.
SLEEVE: Right.
NORM: Okay!
SLEEVE: Okay!
NORM: Can you hear me, Mr. Chuck? (NILES *doesn't.*)
SLEEVE: (*Correctively.*) *Charles!* Can you hear us, Mr. Charles?
NILES: (*New voice; furious.*) Charles Niles, you mental pygmies!
SLEEVE: (*Feigning admiration.*) Very adroit!
NORM: Very adroit! (*Pause.*) *Very!*
SLEEVE: Mr. Niles . . . what comes to mind when you think of wild-eyed radicals who'd steal your income tax money and . . .
NORM: And use it for socialized medicare?
NILES: Gas chamber.
SLEEVE: (*Deliriously pleased, but feigns shock.*) Oh, no!

NORM: (*Same.*) Oh, no!
SLEEVE: (*Feigning horrified concern.*) But what about their wives?!
NORM: (*Same.*) And children?
NILES: (*In fury.*) Let them starve!
SLEEVE: (*Coyly.*) Uh, is it true . . . and I have it on good authority . . . you'd sit back quietly and allow colored folk to move into your neighborhood? (NILES *pauses; they again worry.*)
NURSE: Chuck! He means *Blacks*, that is . . .
NILES: (*Starts angrily to leap from chair.*) Are you out of your *mind?!* You think I'm an idiot? Of course not!!! (*The doctors, arrogant and smug, slowly, triumphantly, step toward footlights and take a stance, swinging their scholarship keys counterclockwise. Lights slowly dim, revealing dawn coming through windows and doors; sound of birds and new morning sounds.*)
NILES: (*Poetic recall.*) Daybreak had begun its reluctant move towards the old adobe by the sea . . . and the first birds began to materialize among the trees. Objects were solid, began to claim shadow . . . and the shadows grew strong and began to assert themselves. (*Pause.*) When finally I awoke, I was pleased to discover that I had become somebody else.
PAULA: (*At bedside.*) Charles . . . how do you feel?
NILES: (*New voice.*) Like a million bucks! (*Pause. Poetic voice.*) I didn't bother to mention that I'd like to have it in unmarked currency, since I might have to steal it. The doctors shook hands with one another and thought of breakfast, possibly laced with 198 proof alcohol. Doctor Sleeve himself gave me his hand. (SLEEVE *does so.*) And inside it was a bill for $998.99.
NURSE: (*Helpfully; cheerily.*) Some of it's for labor, and some for parts. (NURSE *frantically signals to* PAULA *for the money.*)
NILES: (*New, brash voice; eyes the jars on the mantel.*) Yeah! But there's more parts left over than when you started!
PAULA: That's true! The guilt complex! And his Recall!
NILES: (*A harsh, bitter laugh.*) And my conscience! You could recycle it! And pawn it off on some unsuspecting sonofabitch.
SLEEVE: (*A withering glare at* NILES.) And *who* is going to come to *us* for a *conscience transplant?*
NORM: Market's glutted! Right, Miss Thanatopsis?
NURSE: (*Swiftly to mantel where she picks up the jars.*) Here! Be our guest! (NILES *accepts bottles; he stares at them, then at* PAULA *as though asking for an answer.*)
NORM: Nurse! Give him his change. (*To* PAULA.) We knocked off a

couple of bucks because we ran out of antiseptic. We only used . . . (NURSE *vainly signals to* PAULA.)
NORM: (*Interrupts by snatching bill from* NILES's *hand.*) Incidentally, sir, the operation's not tax deductable.
SLEEVE: (*In turn, snatches the bill from* NORM.) Thanks to a bunch of lawmakers with moral hangups! (*He dramatically tears it into small fragments.*) Nurse! Give him his change!
NURSE: (*Nudges* NILES.) Psssssst!
NILES: (*Reacts.*) What's bugging you, sex-bomb?
NURSE: (*Hoarse whisper.*) The *money!*
PAULA: (*Loud, clear, scornful.*) Charles! Give her the money! (*The doctors react to this.* NILES *calmly gets out his wallet. He removes the bills and holds them up for all to see.*)
NILES: You mean, *this?*
SLEEVE: (*Infuriated.*) Nurse! I've told you a thousand times—!
NORM: A thousand times! Never—but *never*—
SLEEVE: (*As they descend upon her.*) Always! Always be sure you—
NURSE: (*Backing away.*) I . . . that is, he . . . (*Passionately, to* NILES.) Chuck! (*She reaches for it,* NILES *dodges.*)
SLEEVE: (*Trying to grab money.*) Look here, sir!
PAULA: Charles! Give them their goddamned money!
NORM: I must warn you, sir! (NILES *has leapt atop the operating table, seizing the power saw enroute. He looks insane, gleeful, and dangerous. they stand around him, uncertain what to do. Freeze position.*)
NILES: They were all staring at me as though I were somebody else. (*He laughs hysterically.*) It was the funniest sight I ever saw. Somehow . . . because I *was* somebody else all right . . . all right . . . all right. (*Pause. The tableau suddenly becomes an active, pleading, shouting cacaphony, mingled with sudden screeching of sea birds, etc.*)
CACAPHONY: Come on Chuck . . . we're all tired . . . He's got a sickness . . . He's not being himself . . . I knew it all along . . . all this lofty hogwash about morals . . . We got witnesses . . .
NILES: (*Gleefully insane.*) So call the police! (*A frightening laugh. He leaps from the table, the power saw still in his hands. He buzzes it threateningly.*)
NURSE: (*The only one not afraid. Embraces him; but convincingly.*) Charley, please! For my sake . . . (NILES *returns the embrace orgiastically—almost.*)
PAULA: Charles! You're sick! (NILES *suddenly releases* NURSE. *He puts*

The Reactivated Man 41

down the power saw and moves ominously toward PAULA *and the doctors. Majestically he tears the money into small shreds and scatters them.*)

NILES: (*He seizes* NURSE's *arm firmly.*) Come on! For your sake! (*He forcefully guides her toward door; she hesitates, almost unsure, glancing at the others — then concurs. Doctors and* PAULA *block doorway, but yield to* NILES's *threatening stance.*)

PAULA: (*Beseeching, a hand on* NURSE's *arm.*) Please! (*She half spins* NURSE *around.*) Do you know what you are doing?

NURSE: (*A low, healthy laugh, sans malice.*) Natch! (*Pause.*) Didn't *you* know what you were doing?

SLEEVE: Nurse!

NORM: Nurse!

SLEEVE: You're hereby fired for unprofessional conduct while on duty! As of now!

NORM: As of *now!*

NURSE: I already quit! Come on, Chuck!

NILES: (*Fumbling in his pockets.*) I am . . .

PAULA: (*Knowing what he seeks.*) The keys! I have them!

NURSE: (*Holds up set of keys.*) The keys! I have them! To Dr. Sleeve's Rolls Royce! (*Laughing,* NILES *and the* NURSE *start through the door.*)

PAULA: Miss! (NURSE *turns; her glance is sympathetic.*) I thought you and I . . . I thought that you . . . (*Breaks off.*) . . . At least you would . . . (NURSE *shows many expressions — sympathy, warmth, sadness, a dismissive shrug.*)

NURSE: Have a conscience? (*She mimes the operation, pointing to her head, churning her hands, and finally with a shrug pointing to one of the jars on the mantel. The theme song is heard. A long pause;* PAULA *glances at* NILES.)

NILES: (*Moves toward* PAULA.) Well? (NURSE *waits: unsure of* NILES *but incapable of insecurity.*) Well?

PAULA: (*A voice of recognition.*) Only the children. (*Pause.*) And part of myself . . .

NILES: (*Soberly, as the* NURSE *watches, he picks up his jar from the table. He professes to examine at arm's length. He tosses the jar which* PAULA *catches.*) Tell them . . . tell *yourself* to always remember . . . this . . . part of myself! (NURSE *breaks out in a shy giggle — not cruel, not childish, but wonderously healthy and innocent. She is joined by* NILES *whose laughter is coarse and harsh, but also healthy and real. The doctors now laugh heartily and long.* PAULA *remains stoic.*

Seeing PAULA's *reaction, the doctors motion for her to get onto the operating table, getting their tools out, with elaborate gestures, preparing for another operation.*

www.ingramcontent.com/pod-product-compliance
Lightning Source LLC
Chambersburg PA
CBHW071802040426
42446CB00012B/2674